Rattle & Numb

Selected and New Poems, 1992-2019

by
John Burroughs

John Burroughs

Dedicated to Dianne Borsenik
without whom infinite flowers
might never have bloomed

CONTENTS

Rattle & Numb: Selected and New Poems, 1992-2019

After Kao Ch'an

this fish aims upward
rises from cooling water
like a fall lotus

John Cage Engaged and Uncaged

Sunken funkin' telepumpkin
Tell a country bumpkin who I am
And then let him tell you

Both will tell it true
Though their perspectives seem contradictory
I'm born of hickory and rectory
Blind Bartimaeus and insightful inspectory
True tale and muddled myth
On an identical trajectory

John Cage or someone like him
(is anyone like anyone
more than anyone is unlike?)
Said disharmony does not exist
Though even we peaceniks are pissed

Corn isn't hominy
But hominy is corn
And care isn't clothing
Though care can be worn
And all can be born
And all can be torn
And loved and forlorn
And warned and scorned
And according to some bother or brother or other
Reborn.

Sunken funkin' telepumpkin
Born of a couch potato
And a pureed tomato
An almost dead and buried berater
Blind hate hater
Lover

Elater
Thin ice skater
War abhorrer
Saint and horror
Mental
And governmental master
Baiter
And sooner or later
Repeat reincarnator.

I am a living death
An awakened dream
Ash unconsumed
And a silent scream
Reconcilable so-called contradiction
And factual fiction

John Cage
Uncaged
Inadequately aged and yet
Timeless
A sublime mess
Subconsciously clothed and consciously undressed
Said worse and better are no less than best
Corn *is* hominy
And there is no disharmony

Only harmonies to which our ears
And our fears
Are unaccustomed

Karma Souptra

Tin can karma
In a cemetery green sedan
Driving into the past
Through the future
Running round and round
And over and over
The illusory track of time
Like a bomb
That never goes off
Like a song that rings
In Campbell's soup cans
Round and round the rims
Not going out or in
Just sticking to the circuit
Like a one ring soup can
Gerbil wheel circus

Till the tin finally erodes
The illusion of time caves in
And full circle
Cemetery green
Karma darts to the next can
In the aisle of now

Bloodshot

Indian summer sun squints,
bloodshot like the wide wounded eyes
of my cynical Seneca ancestors.
On and on and anon,
an endless queue of unrelenting conquistadors,
lusting for booty or bust,
defile our trust and defame the name of God
in the name of God.
Opportunity does not knock for trusting tribesmen,
be they from Arizona, Africa, the Amazon or Akron.
Riding roughshod over every allegedly endless empire
including America the beautifully dutiful,
The cursed hearse of history leads a parade
of pathetic and unsympathetic plotters, plodders,
priests and presidents, electable eels
who feel their forked tongues and dung
make them agents of distinction,
instead of extinction.
Sweetly sighing lullabies of liberty
and expediency,
these leaders open their bomb bays as they pray,
first for the unconditional surrender of their enemies
and last, if at all, for the bloodshot
souls of the soon to be charred
children of Hiroshima, Hanoi
Belfast, Belgrade, Baghdad, Bethlehem
and coming soon to a theatre
of war near you.

RIP

McMahon a dead Ed
Jackson finally beat it
Fawcett stopped running

Media christened
Cosmic Charlie's new angels
Almost born again

TV noose keeps live
Carradine yesterday's news
War children buried

Met a Mat, a Door I Didn't Like

Scribbling
Scrambling
Random ramblings
Run dumb and smart
Numb and smarting
Smarmy
Flush with art and artless
Like farting in calligraphy

Gas rhymes with ass
And no class
And yes
Class
Dismissed rhymes with pissed
And missed and nearly amiss and remiss
Even this

I'm rambling
Randomly scrambling
The few semi worthwhile thoughts I can
Muster with my ass on the toilet
Abdominal cramps
Faux leather journal resting on my write knee
Foster's beer in one hand and
A wine blood red broken but
Functional mechanical pencil in the other

I'm a man
Who doesn't feel like much of one
Not a woman
Though I suppose I feel like most of them

Trying to find myself in
Random scrambling

Rambling
Ambling through a know moon
New moan darkness
Though it's nowhere near midnight yet
And this is one of the year's longest days
Longest daze I've been in for a while
Or so it seems when I'm in it
Trying to bear it
Bare and grin it
Maybe even win it
Or feel like a winner
Instead of a wiener
A whiner or a ham burgher
Though I know I shouldn't treat
This like a competition
Or a smorgasbord

I want to say
What do you know?
But come to think of it
What do I know?
Even my best attempt at avoiding any gimmick
Makes me feel like another dull mimic
Every stab I make at originality
Smells of another stale gimmick
And sometimes my every scribble
Seems to rhyme
With fibble
But in two words
Fib
Bull
And I'm losing any inclination
To play anything other than
Matador

Can Do

On the crapper
Writing shit
Ass agape
On a page not quite
As white as the toilet bowl

I tear off the stinking
Ink soiled sheet
Crumple and drop it
Into the wastewater basket
Flush and retreat

Goodbye cruel word

Do Dew

Half-awake thoughts
Are often the clearest
Unclouded by daydreams
Day schemes
Day screams
Still cool
Gently coated with dew
Soon to be evaporated
Into do

Tell a Vision

Huge oak cabinet console TV
With a broken screen
Sits on the tree lawn
In front of my Cleveland Street house

Took four would be macho men
To get it up the porch stairs and into the living room
Took one might be mouse of a man
With a hand from his wife
To push it out and off
Then down the sidewalk to the curb

She he it
Three major net works
At least one of them
Less high than deaf

Same sidewalk the neighbors' Blazer
Sat blocking today when the police came
Told them to move it
While one of them with an outstanding warrant
Fled out the back basement door
Stumbled his way to a fence behind the house
And barely made it
Over

I in my driveway felt claustrophobic
Not just
Because of the cop car
Blocking my innocent exit

Huge oak cabinet console TV
Been around since at least the early nineties
Till rendered nearly irreparable by rash circumstance
Still feeling mightier than the newer sets

Ahead of its time once
But now more than a decade behind
Wondering if it's obsolete
Or if there's a chance
It's just
Less high than deaf
Eyes been aching
To be rid of this console
For a long bit
And the wife's been aching
For a lighter flatter model
For at least as long

So now it's out on the tree lawn
And even the garbage men don't care
To pick it up

Nearly everyone who passes down
Our busybody street pauses to stare at it
Assess its worth or lack thereof and then move on

I dreamt last night
A strong insightful
Someone stopped
Saw value in our tree lawn trash
Tried her best to push it home
From the end of this claustrophobic driveway
Convinced she could restore it

But I awoke to find
The huge oak cabin net con soul
Remains by the road at the edge
Of this Cleveland Street property
Waiting to be garbage picked
Arrested and destroyed
Retrieved
Rescued
Redeemed

Waiting
Not necessarily wanting
To be the center of attention again
But waiting
To be anywhere except
Anywhere near
That lighter flatter high deaf model
It hears clearly
Inside

Fire, Brimstone

Preacher Gunn
Shoots a yellow green stream
Of ammonia and impurities
Into the white porcelain basin
Of his congregation
Where dehydrated souls
Drink their fill
Of a backward dog's swill

Preacher Gunn
Then runs like a rivulet
Downhill to home
Where he
Loaded and pearl handled
Pukes the hair of a backward dog
On his gun-shy children

Allen Ginsberg Wants You

Allen Ginsberg
You sucked
The cock of life
Drained the bulging bone of its marrow
Homed in on our howling
With your eye on the sparrow
And spit out godly children
A spectacularly spiritual spawn to carry on
Your sacramental work in our wordsick world

A fellatio facial
For earthfolk
Fine and fucked

Allen Ginsberg
Your poetic prick
Penetrated us
Probed the pettiness
Prettiness
Power and pride
Hungrily hardening inside us

Then withdrew to
Spew your gooey godliness
On the just and the unjust
Before turning wholly dust

Orlovsky

I once penned a piece
about Ginsberg loving cock,
should have said Peter.

Identity Crisis

I don't want to be anyone but me
Man
Really
I just want to be all I can be
Until I can't be
Know more
A pure and enduring shooting star
Until it's time to say sayonara
Ka-pow
And ciao

I don't want to be King or Prince
But in another way I do
Since I have a Washington Monument
Full of dreams
Musical schemes
And I know very well
What it's like When Doves Cry
Though I don't have a clue how to answer
The Question of U
(I'm pointing to myself here, too)
And I wonder why it's vice versa
Instead of versa vice

I want to be from the country
And I want to be from town
I want to be the Nowhere Man who
Wherever you go
You find around

I don't want to be Allen Ginsberg
Except when I'm Beat up
Which is most of the time anymore
Though I don't really believe
In time anymore

17

And belief in time is such a chore
When Corso, Kerouac, Cassidy and Burroughs
Are my constant companions

But at times I get terribly tired of feeling Beat
When I'm *On the Road* less than I'm on the commode

I want to go Furthur than Kesey
But I don't want the cuckoo's nest
And I know why the caged bird sings
Though I'm not sure about the rest
Maybe the birds and their songs
And our rights and our wrongs
Are all Maya
In a multitude of hues

The colors run through me
Like a rainbow in an oil slick on an Elyria street
Running through the halls of Marion Correctional Institution
On the eve of the new Millennium
While I watched the 2000 fireworks across the world
On PBS all night long
From my cell
And I wonder
How it's possible I've never been freer
Never been more of a seer than there

And I want to be that free here
Find perfect vision outside of prison

Like it was in the years before and for a while after Bush
In between the ears before and after religion
Tradition
Convention
Ambition
Subtraction and long division
Before and after I was a Skyline Pigeon
With no clue who I was
Or who you were

Or who we are

Maybe I do want to be Ginsberg
Or Kerouac
Coleridge or Kant
Byron
Christ
St. John of the Cross
d.a. levy
Lennon
Martin Luther King, Jr
King Tut
The kid in the cheap seats eating Junior Mints
Wishing he were purple like Prince
Or green like the US Mince
Finally infatuated with the friendship of Peppermint Patty
And earning the love of Lucy
And Desi and the little red-haired girl
And Fred and Ethel Mertz
And Pigpen, Jerry Garcia
Che Guevara, Citizen Kane
And Linus without the line
Or the lie

I don't want to live in vain
I want to be like Steven B. Smith
Maybe Salinger
A .44 Magnum
Not just a Derringer
Johnny Cash, Johnny Carson, Gary Larsen
Tearing down Bergen-Belsen, Washington DC
Garfield and Odie, O.D., and Oh Die
I want to give Peace a chance
But be able to accept that War
Is her partner in the cosmic dance
Accept that both are lies
That nothing in this universe is left to chance
And yet in another sense everything is
And "there's nothing good or bad but thinking makes it so"

But what do I know?

I want to be Dostoevsky without the crime
And especially without the punishment
Have freedom without the army and the government
And I sometimes like to choose
The Karamazov I prefer
And refuse the others
Pretending one brother is better than another

Though I know all too well
That we're all all four Karamazovs
We're all Kazantzakis
Who said "the doors to heaven and hell
Are adjacent and identical"
I think they might be the same door
There may be only one door
We all look at it like blind men looking at an elephant
One grabs the trunk and calls it snake
One grabs the leg and calls it Pillar That Will Not Break
One grabs only a whiff of the tail end
And calls it P.U.

But what is that elephant
Man
Really
With the incredible memory

It's Steven B. Smith
And the firth of fifth
It's Ray McNiece and Tolstoy's *War and Peace*
It's Donald, Dianne, dreams, desire, denial, Demerol
The doomed and the Divine
It's juiced up Roger Clemens saying
Look Babe I didn't share my cigar
With Mark McGwire or Andy Pettitte
It's the heavy and the petty
Jeff Gordon, Dale Earnhardt and Mario Andretti

Racing toward the grave
Slaves of the thrill and the almighty dollar
Kerouac, Ginsberg and Burroughs
Delivering us from literary squalor
Bush and Cheney
And sometimes even Obama
Making us holler
Whitman and Dickinson
Clinton and Monica
Dylan with his harmonica
Clapton and Hendrix with their guitars
Jay Leno with his classic cars
Venus and Mars and Pluto
A big black hole
And a supernova
And so unimaginably much more

I don't want to be any of it
Man
Really
I don't want to be Barack the rock star
Hillary Clinton
John McPalin
Cheech and Chong
Kennedy, Nixon
Mason, Dixon
K-Fed, A-Rod, Brangelina, Britney or Bono
Or do I

I just want to be me
But what is this "me" anyway
What am I
Man
Really

I don't want to be Kipling
Shere Khan, Genghis Khan
An ex-con
The naked Nagasaki bomb bleached Japanese child

The so-called whore in the so-called Nazi Joy Division
Or the so called Not-See in her

I don't want to be the caged bird either
But I want to sing
And I want everyone to listen to my whistling and chirping
Until everyone's bending
And maybe only pretending to listen
Which is probably all they were ever doing in the first place
Bending
Pretending to hear
Man
Really

And me too
Though I try like the Devil not to
I pretend to listen and then wonder what I'm missing

Maybe the whole shebang is a lie
Mighty Maya
Caged birds, songs and all
Because how free can we really be
Man
Really

How free in the land of the penny pinch
And the US Mince
And poetry turned know-it tree
Or no-it tree

It's all bleeding like a sappy lie
Sticky sweet
Through the crimson streets
And in our futile funk
We tap the trunk
Try very hard to refine or define the oozing goo
Yet it's totally true, too
All too real
And there's nothing *more* real in this whole ordeal

We call the universe

It's all illusion
It's all allusion
And it's all there is

Kurt Cobain sang "All in all is all we are"
But he did not believe it
Said the gun
And if there's no fun in the pretense
If there's no *joi* in the *vivre*
Then we might as well leave
And maybe someone who sticks around will be happier

I want to be Faithwalker
And sight walker
Oblivious to and aware of every hurdle
I want to be Theresa Göttl
Stretching the window from out of the desert
To be like Hansel and Gretel
Eating their gingerbread house
And being tasted and tested but not consumed
To impress all the chaps
And even perfect bound books
Like Larry Smith and Mark Kuhar
But be the Top Dog
Deeper than Cleveland
Like a Jim Thome homer back in the day
Finding its way to the bottom of Lake Erie
And beyond
To be professors like Howard Ellis, Timothy Leary
John McKenna, Helen Shepard
And the Good Shepherd
The innocent shepherd boy blue
With the sheep in the meadow and the cow in the corn
And a Satchmo horn that I can blow like Miles
And a free pass to get me through
The most expensive turnstiles
And the aisles and aisles and miles

Of poetry in your eyes

I want to be like my wife Geri Lynne
Like my mom again
Like my grandchildren
Like my dad
Like my dear old granddad
But without the nasty Nazi tattoo on his hand
I want to maintain a bad boy image
Without having anyone mistake me for bad
To keep them from messing with me
Without keeping them in fear
And maybe then I won't be so sad
Around here

I want to have a certain semblance of madness
To infuse and inspire my art
But I don't want people to take me too seriously
When I appear to fall apart
Or think I'm really mad except in the most brilliant of ways

And I guess that what I want most these days
Is out of this daze I've been in
Since God-knows-who knows when

I'd like to be able to start again

I want to know who I actually am
And to be it
I want folks to see it
Man
Really see it
And not judge it and hopefully love it
And be what they are and love it
And I'll love it too

There's a part of me that believes I'm really you
And yes, you're really me
And if we could just open our egotistical eyes and see it

We could love
Man
Really
And maybe love would be all we need after all

And I don't think things would get too terribly boring
With all this love and no warring
As long as we didn't all live forever
And overpopulate the earth
To the point that we suck her dry and
Destroy our chances of living at all

But we're doing that already anyway
And I wonder if our birth and being
Really complement the earth we're seeing
Or condemn it

And while we're feeling up the elephant in the room
Blind as bats and batty as Babe Ruth
We mistake the lie for truth and truth for lie
We swallow maxims like an "eye for an eye"
And wonder why we can't see
Maybe there is nothing real or untrue
But thinking makes it me
And makes it you

I suspect I know all too well
That each of us is all four Karamazovs
In handwritten Russian heavens and hells
And Nabokovs
Molotovs
Kerouacs jacking off
We're all Mandela and Frederick Douglass and Crazy Horse
Stephen Biko and the Velvet Underground and Nico
Zorba the Greek and Nikos Kazantzakis
Who said in *The Last Temptation of Christ* that
"The doors to heaven and hell
Are adjacent and identical"

I'm willing to bet my chances at either-or
That they're just the same door
That there might be only one door after all
And we're all pretending to see it
Like blind men looking at an elephant

One grabs the trunk and calls it a snake
One grabs the leg and calls it Pillar That Will Not Break
One grabs only a whiff of the tail end
And calls it P.U.
But we fail to see it be you
And be me as much as it be him or her
Or B.M.

And all in all is all we are
Like Kurt Cobain said before he blew off his head
All in all is all we are
Despite our poetry
Or know-itry or no-itry
And one day we will know it
See
And if Kurt didn't really believe it all before
He said ciao and ka-pow
He does now

Out and In Audible

Every act of creation
is an erasure
an abrasion
an anaphylactic
shock and awe
hack job
a pleasure
wrought of leisure
and an irrepressible
need to blather on
both with and without
words.

Every devastation is
an act of creation
is an act
of transfusion
and a letting of blood
rich jewel confusion
a measure
of destruction
in the symphony
of what is becoming
a disillusion
of what is not
et voilà
a twat shot full of love
a love of splatter
a shortage
and abundance
of what we call sanctity
and insanity
in and out
of fertile matter.

Every creation is
an act of destruction
and reproduction
a deconstruction
of yesterday
but a recreation
of tomorrow
an ablation
sullied only by illusion
a transmission
in search of substantiation
contracted
into transubstantiation
expanding like
an outstanding ovation
both with and without
reason
a scene
both with and without
cohesion
both in and out
of season
both over
and under
heard.

I Hear Change

I hear
the only
thing you
can ever be
sure of is
change.

I hear
change
is

eternal.

But try telling that
to a dollar bill.

My BIOS

In the middle of BS
I owe.

Mercy Less

Listening to Love
by the dash board reflection
of sunlight filtered
through my Buick windshield
waiting for High
Me to emerge
from some medical office
affiliated with a hospital
in Oberlin
recently renamed
Mercy.

Her real name
though perhaps more prosaic
is easy to figure
if you're halfway familiar
with mangled Spanish.

But this is not 1966
Love has long
since disbanded
and I arrive home
to find a letter
from an attorney
representing the hospital
notifying us he's moved
the court for a default
judgment.

Still ill
I call it *despiadado*
merciless in English
recall I forgot
my CD in the car

And she asks
Where's the Love?

Kiss

You pronounce *les jardins*
like lay jar don
but I find the way you pout
your lips and curl
your tongue as you enunciate
sweet evidence
that your other French
is exquisite.

Come Pass

East and west
collide and mesh
in ways no mechanical
device can measure.

There is no true
north or south here
only our spiraling toward
what is and seems
meant to be.

Heart needles spin
like clock hands
but swifter and
less certain.

I take my direction from you.

Cannot Believe William S. Burroughs Is Dead

Dream
Spectral old man
Gaunt
Beside me
In a large
Late sixties sedan
North on route 57
Through mid-Ohio
75 miles an hour
No other cars
Of the accelerator he says
"Hit it like you
Live—HARD"
When whoa!
A sign directly in front of us
Says LEFT
But there's no control
In the steering wheel and
Foot still on the gas
We launch
Straight into the sign
No matter what
Go forward
Awaken.

Alarm Blocks

I awoke with a stack
of bricks on my chest
bloody dull red blocks
forming a hard slimy
semiconscious ark
and it was death to touch
as seen in Exodus
after the flood in Genesis
where two of every species
wooden stallions
stone night mares
weighed on my horse sense
and sanity and eye
screamed sanctify me
but I was already a saint
as well as a sitcom
a sixties love song
steeped in dung
steeple chased
because some animal
church wants to make me
foxtrot in tempo
with the braying
boy Pinocchio
wants to make me
hog its slops like
Pigpen McSomething
grateful and dead
wants to make me change
the litter in its offering box
as I swill from and fill it
like chairman meow
dogsick beyond the ability
of any Dramamine

or drama there
to keep me from falling
into the who of you better
you bet I stuck cotton
up my nose while thinking
this whole dream
has to be real because
it smells funkier
than red white and blue
shorts on James Brown
in a cold sweat
in a rocky screenplay
set to feature Sylvester Stone
singing Family Affair
and I awoke with a stack
of four children
on my chest and
four adults had us covered
nearly smothered
trying to put us out
and back to sleep
perchance to scream
sometimes I screech
like a mystical magpie
only to awaken again
in muffled madness
recalling funerals
follow many wakes
and this is why I need
not set the alarm clock
and always try to sleep
on top of the blankets.

Electric Miasma

John Burroughs is something
like an indeterminately charged
deep press ion
positive or negative
depending on which way
the wind's particles blow.

North Pole
South Pole
Godsend
asshole.

I sore
with rhymes
eye poor
at times
son visor
daughter miser
Kublai Kaiser
word up riser
untoward down player
getting grayer
and grayer
and eventually gayer
with or without
your little pills
teeming landfills
achtung hills
bone mills
TV swill
Jack and Jill Amityvilles
three and a half Mendelssohns
and Camp Pendeltons

So up end someone

and call me him
or him me if you will.

Still
I'm something
like an indeterminately charged
deep press ion
no see icon
rhyme addict
line scion
cowardly lion
lying in a meadow
full of leaves
of grass
saying to my up
and down poles
I'm Walt
wit man
my ass.

Tell Them I Am Sent You

I am

sitting next to words I can't hear
hearing words I can't sit next to
day dreaming
nearly nodding

I still

reach to my right
grab a random book from the shelf
notice its Ferlinghetti title
Wild Dreams of a New Beginning
open it at random to page 22 slash 23
"Snapshot Epiphany"

I am now

contemplating my great effort
to break away from using gerunds
realizing how difficult it can be
to resume
recalling that point 22 is a gun
that 23 was a Cavalier small forward
and famed Bull shooting guard

I find myself

putting the book back
on its black shelf with Homer and Frost
distracted by deep impressions
depressed to my distraction
unsuccessfully resisting an impulse
to rhyme with satisfaction

The poem is not really
disintegrating

I am

still
now

Magnetic Repulsion

I build liquid sound bruises
from a blue book stagger
slice love song summers
into dirty skin showers
blossom slender immense
burning

Ask how you can
see smell tell
use work grow
consume bomb
bouquet

Crack glass
say go
let leave

A Poem Like John Dorsey
—by Sod Dummy

I want to write a poem in John Dorsey's style
so Dylan will call *me* an underground man
I want to write a poem like John Dorsey
just to prove I can
But would John Dorsey be caught dead
writing in rhyme
even half the time
and anyway I don't have a Rocky
Balboa tee-shirt to wear under my sport coat
and I can't find orange pants
or a fuzzy top hat like his anywhere
and the Collingwood Arts Center
in Toledo where he lays his head
reminds me of the piano tuning school
I lived in when I was 18
It used to be a YMCA
and when the last student graduated
and the owner died his daughter
who was every bit as hot
as my second grade teacher
dismissed the students
sold the pianos
padlocked the communal kitchen
and allowed the City of Elyria to tear it down
to make room for a Justice Center

I want to write a poem like John Dorsey
But when I see the name Toledo
I think of a painting by Goya
which reminds me of how our forefathers
taught us to mispronounce *Toledo*
and unlike John
I never met Gregory Corso
and I made myself forget

the time my mom asked me if I was gay
and I had to Google *Swank* magazine
and D.E. Oprava probably won't publish my book
and I haven't finished writing it anyway
and Scott Wannberg and S.A. Griffin probably won't care
to write one with me
and I don't give one flying fuck
about Harvey Keitel
let alone three
I'm my own actor
even if I've never spent a night in Los Angeles
or New York City
or in Tremont watching the moon come out
on Steve Goldberg's balcony
and I may never read in the Bowery Poetry Club
or have the balls to take a bus
to Kansas City or California
or co-host a reading with Michael Grover
and I hate gummy bears
and though I thought myself well acquainted
with the ins and outs of Sodomy
I needed John Dorsey
to tell me it's a city in New Jersey

It's not easy being a word-boxing stallion
like John Dorsey
going the distance with Apollo
knocking out Creed in the sequel
It's not easy getting into a ring with Mister T
or following James Brown
especially with a Cold War win
only to windup broke again
coaching Tommy Morrison
before returning to the ring
in unparalleled form in *Rocky VI*
And I'm not even sure I'm up to
being the heavyweight champ
peen of poetry like John Dorsey
as long as that building in Elyria

where the piano tuning school used
to stand is called a Justice Center
and anyway trying to write
a poem like someone else
is so unlike John Dorsey
So instead I'll be content to call him my friend
have a few laughs with him at our mutual expense
and everywhere I go
love him like a brother
except maybe
in New Jersey

Cover Girl

I want to drink a dream or two with you
not just dream and drink separately
somewhat desperately like I used to do
before I knew of you
and a little while after.

I want to sink with laughter
into the drain of you and
return from over the brink
of ecstasy with you next to me
before we slink off to sleep and keep
each others' nightmares at bay
like we've tried to do all day
but this time more restfully
and successfully.

I want to sleep with
the taste of you all over me
and the taste of me in you.

And though I used to believe
I'd need and want more
the thought of sharing and being
unsparingly dowsed in all that comes
with your dream drain drink
makes me think dearest lover
that you've got it all covered.

Dish Work
—recalling Columbia Hills Country Club, 1986

Geri was a waitress
served me a stiff drink called a screaming orgasm:
vodka, Irish cream, amaretto and coffee liqueur.

While soaked in steam from the dishwashing machine
I scrubbed dried hollandaise sauce
from some would-be PGA star's lunch plate
and waited for *our* lunch break
in the basement storeroom where we'd covertly
wash down the day's eggs Benedict with another.

But this time no screaming.

A Taste of Heaven

Your golden hair halo
above as below illuminates
all I'm inclined to know
renders sunlight redundant
while the scent of your wrist
and the touch of the back
of your knee and all
they surround and entail
never fail to keep me astir in
a day and night dream state
of hunger and thirst for
the next time your erotic
nectar graces my tongue.

O T

I sit in the sun on my back patio
drinking the last of Geri's white wine
watching her plant a foxglove
bending over.

There's a jar of dried pennyroyal leaves
just inside on our basement shelf.
I've been thinking of making, oh, tea of it
for two or three years.

Why haven't I?
Maybe I'm afraid
of leaving.

So I sit drinking the last
of Geri's white wine and
wonder if she'll even notice
what she'll say if she does.
I imagine she's tired of my whine
wishing or afraid I'll tire of hers.

Until then,
bottoms up.

Bier

Beer is a beauty
Beer is a bitch
Beer is a scratch for my vilest itch
An itch for my finest scratch
A down the hatch batch of high satisfaction
A recipe for extreme stupefaction
A flood disguised as a dream panacea
And whether or not I wish to see it
A slow tide of suicide

The blue moon is high
And the beer sea is strong
As I down another and continue this
Song swell without a tune
This sickeningly sweet I scream sundown
Melting as I search
For a silver spoon that does not exist
In a glass of whatever's on tap
Getting pissed
Fancying myself an inimitable wordsmith
While I wanly regurgitate yesterday's news
My blues rhyming with brews
And still thirst unquenchably
For the deluge to deliver me
To low dry land
And sober death

Dry Cast

I've got water on the brain but can hardly translate it
into words I believe can quench your thirst
whether in the Sudan or northeast Ohio.

I've got water in my veins and I'd gladly bleed
to satisfy your worthy need if I believed
it would do the trick and I could survive the loss.

Okay maybe I do and maybe I can
but I'm as afraid of bloodletting as I am to believe that
there could be water enough to keep you alive in these syllables
when my spirit seems dryer than ash and blowing toward death.

But though I fall apart
my limbs like embers put out by winter
my blood escaping prodigally onto the barren February earth
where my favorite pen lies half rusted and half frozen
I pick it up and attempt to get as much of my blood as possible
onto paper in the form of words and get them to you
perceived inadequacies and all
before both they and we dry out completely
rendering our water words and translation obsolete.

Numb And

number
number
number

in your case
6 channels
3, 5, 8, 19, 25 and 43
through 1 antenna
900 channels via cable
9 DVDs on the mantle
32 flavors
4 scoops tonight
and like me you become

number
number
number

in my case
24 cans
a 6 pack
3 20-ounce tallboys
a 40
4 pints
1 shadowed love
and all this
in 2 weeks

in 2 weaks
who seek strength
in numbers

Peacing It Together
—after U2

there is no line on my horizon
but there's no horizon on my line either

i'm still piecing together this puzzle
that's never really been apart
except through my own narrow too-close perception

on an atomic level with all these hard-to-see electrons
spinning in apparent chaos and non-thought about me
it's easy to feel my whole u 'n' i verse is out of control

but from a broader perspective it seems the electrons
protons and neutrons are all in their proper places
making oxygen possible
which in turn combines
with hydrogen to make water possible
which in turn makes me
who in turn makes these words fluid
or tries to do it

i suppose any line i see on the horizon
between atom and eve would be illusory
as it is between morning and eve
between birth celebration and death grieving
between coming maybe coming again and leaving
between unwittingly revealing the truth
and intentionally deceiving
between you and me even
and what seems outside of us
and not about us and still somehow about us after all

i'm still piecing together this puzzle
that's never really been apart
any more than the sea and sky on my horizon

sea part of sky after all
evaporating
forming and filling clouds
clouds and more
clouds dissipating
and falling again as rain
rinse and repeat
rinse and repeat

no matter how many times i shampoo my mind
i find myself all wet
like last night's dishes soaking in the sink
waiting for me to get to washing them
hot water turned cold and feeling greasier
than it did last night
not making the dishes any easier
and here i am trying to write a poem
thinking maybe there's no line
between this poem and those dishes
in the sink of my life
wondering who i am in this analogy after all
the silverware
the poem
the dishrag
the pots and pans
the water
the grease flowing from one to the other and back
and eventually down the drain
or this whole kitschy sink
drink and all

and even when i can no longer function
i wonder whether i will outlast
this crumbling house about me
for it seems there is only a man
made line between sink and house
between functioning not functioning and simply being
between washing last night's dishes

and this morning's poetrying
washing last night's poetry and this morning's dirty ass
between this and that
those and these
utilizing my legs and utilizing my knees
wiping this poetic plate with the last
one's electrons protons and neutrons
hydrogen oxygen hydrogen
dirty cleansing water
and words

i fish for my favorite poetic cup
catching another i like as well
but never catching the horizon i hear tell
is in there out there somewhere
sure as hell is unsure as i
because the only hell imaginable is one we imagine
and i just can't choose between earth and sea
and sky when as far as i can tell
there is no line on the horizon
between any or all of them
or between any or all of them and me

but i'm willing to concede
that as far as i see isn't necessarily all there is
so i keep my line in the dirty
cleansing dish water of this u 'n' i verse
fishing for clear categories
though there's been no horizon on my line yet
and as far as I can tell there never will be

i've had my hands and hook in this
sink for fifty-odd years so far
rinse and repeat
rinse and repeat
and for what
maybe because i'm a poet and the sink is my poetry
or because I'm human
and the sink is my me

and maybe this is why i feel so often like i'm sinking

but if you look at the world upside down...

and who's to say which side is up
an ohioan's upside down is an australian's right side up
and from the sun's perspective there is no line
between right side up and upside down
it's all the same
because the sun's eyes aren't just on one end of his body
his hands aren't just on a compass or clock
like ours

so i often feel like i'm sinking
but if i look at the world upside down
which from a broader perspective is
no different than right side up
i see that as much as i'm sinking i'm also rising
and so are you

there is no horizon on our line
and there's no line on our horizon

we're still piecing together a puzzle
that's never really been apart

Loveshot

I want to push into you
my fear of pushing into you
but not infect you with
a fear of being pushed
too hard

I want to plunge all my poetry
into the toilet of us 'til we rise
flush and brimming with words
unspoken to tear pages from
the book of our fecal pasts
and burn them for warmth

I want to marry you
without burying you
kiss you without our lips
ever having to part and
leave the resulting mess
for someone else

I want to stoke your silver engine
stream past you like a highway
wash over you like a river
take back everything I didn't give you
just to store it up for the rainy days
after I retire from commitment
and you move on to Tom
Dick or someone scarier

I want to die and be reborn
as a rock, star, geologist, astronomer
I want to orbit you like a moon
but not always show you my best side
want to blaze like a comet
break free from my circuit

plunge into you
burn out in your atmosphere

I want what you are
in ways you won't want long
and ways years later I hope
you'll still want strong

I want to fire my
arrow into you
and quiver

Halfwet Dream

I drank the whole bottle
knowing we
cannot know all
each other.
I'm cruising
for a brew sin,
used to walk about
with a group to pull
ourselves past to the end,
just to find us now
hapless half laughing
visionaries murmuring
who and how.

Green Heart

Absinthe is not an electronic keyboard you play with your midsection muscles but a green liquor sleeping with wormwood stashed behind the Zohar in my basement bookcase. In this case, brand name Absente, it's 136 proof and came with its own golden slotted spoon you can rest on your glass, liquor on the bottom, sugar cube on the top. Pour water slowly over the sugar 'til it dissolves, turning the liquid white and cloudy, then pour the concoction slowly down your throat until your fear and occasional paranoia dissolve into white cloudy apparent clarity.

Last night I couldn't be with you, so I opened the bottle, surprised how much it smelled like licorice, tasted like ouzo but smoother, probably because wormwood numbs the tongue like cocaine, and got high on the thought of you and the thought of the feel of you and the feel of the green then white and cloudy liquid that took me to you or away from feeling you absent and reminded me what I love and don't always love but sometimes miss about loving you. As I poured a second glass of green and dissolved a second sugar cube over it into further white cloudy apparent clarity, a thought occurred to me, sending me to find my journal and write it down. Absinthe makes the heart fonder.

Piss on Arson

He's tired of competition
tired of the fire it takes to sometimes win
tired of firemen's balls and forced grins
black sooty booty calls and hairpin turns of conscience
tired of the collateral damage they can cause.
He knows sometimes it takes competition
to bring out the best in folk but fuck
if it doesn't also bring out the worst
and burn the dry woulds in every direction
and on closer inspection he wonders
what weapons fashioned by fiery men
are worth in the water hose long run.

(Therefore?) I Am

If I were an old sage
And knew I'd die tomorrow
What would I say tonight?
Maybe this:

Don't believe a word of it
Even the most honest and well-intentioned
Is on some level
And perhaps all
A lie

I love you more than you know
And less than you think
Depending on who you are
And how much I've had to drink

But I love you all
I'm sure of it
I want to be sure of it
I think

Horror Scope

My horoscope says
be part crocodile, part bird.
I fear I'll eat me.

Top Less

I'm feeling topless
or longing to feel
top less, I'm not
always sure which.

I want to remove the lid
from my cranium.

This might require surgery
a letting of blood
a sawing through bone
some alone time.

This might require a fire
that burns through
skeletal matter
without adversely
affecting the brain
beneath that
I believe
I think
matters most.

Grab your dusty hat
throw it on the fire with mine—
have to let brains breathe.

Keyed Up

I'm so keyed up I can't write good poetry
can't be dispassionate
can't be compassionate
so stressed out because
you don't want me here
I don't want you here
and yet we remain
and complain
and complicate our common pains
with blame and shame
and rainless thunder
rattling our home and bones
dryer and dryer
like a ring full of keys
in a doorless desert
thirsting for somewhere to fit
longing to unlock more
than words of love

You key me deeply
I key back

You almost break my car door handle
trying to keep me from driving away

I twist your wrist as I make my escape
only to drive around the block
sit awhile in the parking lot
across the street
then gently jingle back into the house
after dark
to see you pretend
you're glad to see me again
seeming like I missed you
and can't live without you

I missed *something*
but I'm not sure what

I miss some things
I've grown accustomed to going without

I miss nothing—or at least little
besides the illusions I used to keep
the nights I used to sleep
in a cell I could comprehend
in a hope you could not upend
in a dream I thought I'd never rip to shreds

I'm so keyed up I can't write good poetry
though I like to believe
(this gets better as it goes)
I'm just not sure
(if I ever was)
I'm not pure
(though I never was)
I only want to love and be loved
or feel
at least
that I love and am loved

I don't want to feel much else
but I feel *everything* else
can't be dispassionate
can't be compassionate
thunder is torment
rain thirst is torture
and letting us live like this can't be love

If I'm wrong
hate me

Unlock us up
and throw away the keys

Out (Not Fade Away)
—after Neil Young

I did what I did and I knew what I knew
and it all came to nothing

Maybe if I did what I knew and knew what I did
it would have come to something
but then again maybe I
both knew and did
long before I was young
and it still came to nothing

What's new?

Someone with no clue how to fix his or her life
told me how to fix mine
gave me some books or records they thought
divine sublime or something of the sort
and whether I took their advice or not
it all came to naught
like when I played
wreckereds or gave books
to other folk
who thought
they were nothing

They just folking
stared
maybe the extra are
in scarred
or out
our scared

Though I could not

tell front from behind
the pearls from swine
before I knew what it meant
to kneel I gave
my advice a swell
I gave ad
I gave vice
I gave sugar and spice
naughty and nice
head to the shoo
and it all came to something
resembling little
more than anything at all
but me and you

Who am I fooling?

No matter how many
worlds of words I put it into
it still comes to nothing

I traded in my bicycle for care
my care for a car
my car for another car
my other better car for the same old bicycle
and this endless cycle for more care
but it all came to nothing

I read books and did chores
distinguished between bores
and boars and boors
but could never extinguish
wars and worse

And though I tried to rush her
all I did was hush her
perhaps even crush her but
I could never crush hearses
and they still came

to nothing

I wrote and I wrote
and I typed and I typed
I wrote about this type or that
I typed about this rote or that
rotor this
wrote her that
and it all turned to piss
or even less
till no one in particular
hit the flusher and it all
went to shit

But in spite of it I wrote on
rode on
right on
wry dawn
rite yawn

It all grew tired
unwired
beautifully turned dutifully
and mutually undesired
until untied began to end up
reminding me of united
except out of order
and unrequited

In other words
it all came to nothing

When I found myself
just pulling the levers
trying to be clever
dying to be better
and better at dying
I wondered what's the use trying?
it all comes to nothing anyway

Why not shut up and let it
and try to forget it?

I drove tanks into banks
and I drank and I drank
and I sank and I stank
and it all came to nothing

I sat sober two decades
even then I decayed
and grew more and more dismayed
as it all fell apart
and even my heart
and hard drive came
to nothing

So I finally gave up
figured fuck the indoors
I'd make love to the outdoors
never mind the chores
try having a sun
who unlike me could successfully run
from everything that comes to nothing
including this cold old earth
and myself

If I had to succumb
I'd at least go out feeling
enlightened and warm
at least go out feeling like something
hotter than cold
more young than old

So the sun starts blazing
and coming out of yore
and my haze I know
longer wish two
earn and yearn

my way too
a wormy grave

Blast being grounded
give me an urn

Kneel young, right?

It's better to burn

Going Mobile
—a title as redundant as I sometimes feel

Often I feel I
overthink
most everything I do or say.
Other times I feel I don't
think enough
or am thoughtless.
Sometimes I feel I'm doing
or not doing
both simultaneously.
It's enough to render me immobile
like the main man in John
Barth's *The End of the Road*.
That's when by sheer force of will,
whether it's a waste
of energy
and time
or not,
I make myself remain mobile,
at least in
this three-ring
gerbil wheel circus—
because I feel
if I'm not
doing *something*,
I might as well
stop.

Tooth Telling

I wanted badly
to bite the slight
bulge of belly beneath
your navel.

But I feared
you might
bite back.

Slipping Backwards into Blue Eden

She drew me into the Cain and Abel
and into the under the table and
dreaming *I* was in a Dave Matthews
video I crashed into a melodic yearning
for burning harmonies yet unheard.

She drew me into the bird and bush
and sent me scattered into the cold
garden air like a serpent's sycophant
falling tail first down a psychic staircase
and the way she stared at my wasting
shivers sent splinters up my tree of knowledge
until I forgot why I felt the fig leaves necessary.

Align

If I were to kiss you
in Strongsville, Ohio,
in front of the picture
window at Borders Books,
would you think I crossed
the man made line between
should and could and would,
the three dimensional line
between before and behind?
Would you curse me blind
or be kind?

More than Sax

She says our worlds
keep colliding
and she says go with it
John just let it flow
write it as it comes
and she says I love you
and please
enjoy your day.

I'm listening
to Rahsaan Roland Kirk
playing Misty
and I Want Talk
and I want you
though you wear many faces
just like me and
how can I love one
and not the others?

Perfection Per Fiction

To err is human, to air is divine—
so I think sometimes—
but other times I struggle
to find a clear line between the two.

Anyway God,
if he or she did or didn't
fill the Bible with hot air—
check the etymology of inspire—
didn't seem to stop it
from becoming a red herring.

Maybe the desire to be perfect—
that is, other than what we are, human—
is the true error.

Maybe we know what we know,
don't know what we don't know,
know what we don't know and
don't know what we know
all at the same time.

If to err is human
and a human ways him or herself
on another's idea(l) of balance
and is no longer found wanting,
is his or her perfection then an error,
a low turn on the high weigh of humanity?

Maybe *I'm* full of hot air.

Maybe being human is our perfection
and divinity is fiction.

Maybe our need to be perfect—
wrought of our obsession with seeing
humanity,
error,
humanity in error,
error in humanity—
is the true red herring,
of which the Bible's (and/or our) air/err
are but too scales.

A Wrinkle in Time

Rip Van Wrinkle is about to be pressed
under an incredible weight of cold
someone else's warm gold
until his celestial unconsciousness
and terrestrial conscience
awaken in vicious yet voluptuous time.

Rip Van Wrinkle knows not his place of birth
his purpose on earth
but what concern is that
to a man who wanders dimly
by turns glibly and grimly
across broken dream pavements
through heretofore unmapped brambles?

Rip Van Wrinkle gambles
that he cannot fail to uncover
the dismal yet fortunate truth
which in the manner of many before
he might overlook in a restless quest
to confirm his suspicion that somehow
all or none of this is his or god's mission
though he doesn't see much difference.

...When finally the last
of the gold has been mined
and the press loses its icy heft
Rip Van will awake and thaw
arise from a decade largely undecayed
and purposefully drive on
a bolder and wiser
unapologetically irrepressible
Wrinkle.

CRYst

I'm a messiah
with emphasis
on the first syllable

Christ
with a y and no h
and the first three
letters capitalized

Mess
sigh
ugh

Deep Seated

I sit in Kohl's parking lot
listening to U2's Elevation
thinking about my West Virginia roots
trying to dig myself out

Being the Change Is Not Enough

I change every year, every day
and so does everyone else.
And why do we change these ways
if this isn't what we wish to see?
Maybe we have no choice.
We do each have a voice but
maybe that's not enough either
and maybe we need to use it or
maybe we need to stop and not
just be something but do it.

I admire much about Gandhi
and on the surface his saying
"be the change you wish to see
in the world" sounds beautiful.
But Bush wished to see two
wars and tax cuts for the rich who
wanted to see themselves richer
while Bin Laden wished to see
buildings full of people destroyed
and Hitler wished to see millions
of eyes and wishes exterminated.

Telling a hungry mother to be
the change she wishes to see
is like telling her to be the meal
she wants to eat and the money
that'll pay her family's heating bills
and as long as she can hardly
afford her latest baby's formula
Gandhi's will not satisfy.

Way Erred Scenes Inside a Jazz Mine

Aswirl in creative flux
feel a faux need to squeeze
to get any err out
on screen or page
feeling sage in this smoke
of jasmine incense
hearing a catalyzing muse
sick I can't name and
I can't blame
you or blame me
not sure why we need to lay
it on anyone
as it is what it is
and just is
and what's wrong with that
why do we
always have to find something
wrong with everything
I can sing
without notes or tune
and so
I suspect
can you
whether or not some see it
as cruel or kind
aren't we blind to believe
every song needs sound waves
every lyric needs words
every world needs saved
every who needs heard
every herd needs a who
ain't it just what it is
whatever it is

and I know Dylan
said he not busy being born
is busy dying
but he failed to say
he busy being born is busy dying too
and why can't we say that
unafraid
it is what it is
and so what
the best jasmine incense burns out
and the worst lives
in memory just as long and wise
any writer wrong
what's worst or best
anyway
scents won't last forever
I think nonsense
won't either
but in some sense might
like night
wonder
if one day everything
we think is wrong
passes on
and everything right is left
could anything be right again
without us rewriting it
and when
you or I wonder
why I do or don't talk
may be hear's what you're missing
I'm always listening
and never shut up
sure it's easy to think
at least one of us is
in this walled room
in this sided house
in this incorporated city in this state

of apparent confusion
but Daishonin said
ichinen sanzen
each moment possesses three
thousand realms
and I'm never outside a moment
even when I'm conscious
and your movement pervades
the realms I monitor
even when you don't feel
odd when you don't hear
sometimes we use the wrong ears
wrong might be the wrong word
because in certain uncertain worlds
sound waves are inefficient
often ineffectual
and even oddly misleading
despite their repeated best intent
shuns to be otherwise
so I use them or don't
you too
as inclination dictates or allows
but it's all
now
becoming
evident to me
that we're all ultimately
aswirl in creative flux
insight
outside
out of sight
inside
becoming
okay
either way
with or without
hour
foe need
two squeeze

smoke key
jazz mine

Lit (Er, a Tour)

I. SEE

At the Literary Café
I tap at my HP laptop
just in from the back room
where Tremont's self-named
Pretentious Artists are
drawing Geri's portrait

Too many people showed up
to draw for my pretentious
computer and me to fit
so I sit at the bar with
a goblet of Samuel Adams
drafting this poem
happy for an excuse
to watch the proprietor
draw me another

If this were not Cleveland
but Bar Harbor, Maine
Hinkle Mountain
Cemetery even
Hell, Michigan
I might not tell you
that I know what it's like
to be dead and I know
who I am when dead
more than I do when alive
when my shirt's off
and the jailhouse tattoo
around my navel shows
faded black

I need a vacation
from gesticulation
from this bonanza
of kicks and scarred tricks
and the makeshift matrix
that began as a poet tree and
seems to have been licked
and chipped into a crucifix
for your chewing and
spewing measure

I crave a break from vanity
and my own worst enemy
and this ear-grabbing Bowie
both the now playing Fame
and the knife

So I sit at the bar
in your Literary Café
considering drawn lines
that do and don't compute
quietly and methodically
freaking out and feeling
both more and less gray
both swifter than fascination
and slower than incarceration
both lower than a sucker
and higher than a fuck you
can easily lead my blood
both more and less
you than me and
truer than what
you might expect
in the face
of this illusion
and disillusion

I wane and wax well

literate and ill
iterate my compulsion
to get with it or to hit it
like the road not as
faultless as I seem
rowed by forces I can't name
and unsure both at sea
and on shore

I try scraping the sky
take pride in my architecture
exaggerate my height but
tend to sink and erode and
aspirate undrawn water when
thrown in certain literary streams
because that's what you seem to expect
of the buildings you've helped erect
of this half sentient sandstone

Every door
every drop
every more
every spinning top
every stop on the
marriage-go-round
every button on my shirt
is a hiding from hurt

Now I'm tired
out of cash
my last glass is empty
and so we head home together

Her portraits are finished
almost suitable
for naming

Mine are not

II. LEAVE

if you want to
I don't need you
I've pretense
us-ness to spare
bela double
toil and treble
bass and waste
a briefly pretty
face and a haste
to erase
every place
I've ever known

I grow wild and beautiful
lift light from under stones
roam where I want to
leave where I sit
shit steamy
sleep dreamy
recall creaming Cassie
who I met through Melissa who
listened to Eno and Fripp
and made me lose my grip
like Rael by the pound
and sounded like larks'
tongues in Telekon
served with lamb on Broadway
hand over my basket
ball for the bliss of Exposure
and a kiss under Evening Star
a Numan inexplicably
loving Collins' feel

I jumped pre-1984
into the fountain

named after her
found her later
at the mall with my real gal
left the latter and reconnected
with Melissa in downtown Elyria
and never gave a thought
to see leave land
where my mom worked
at the psych hospital

I loved her efficiently
across from the high school
till she heard about my black
girlfriend and ended things
and got with the guy
who became Daniel's father
before I wondered whether
I was dad and she had
second thoughts
about us both
not Daniel

I found her later
at the gay bar in Lorain
loved her again
whirled and shared
like our word children
my black faux brother
my bisexual red haired lover
on Gulf Road
and she gave me
my second hit
of LSD and though
I continued to leave
I began to see further
into the mouth of what
Cleveland might be

She was my introduction

to poetry while she wrote
and my graduate course
when she quit

She was my it
and but and or
my Marillion and
uncountable millions
and more as our gulf
widened and finally broke

Wreck her
she was all that music
and I was her once

I cry because
I can't
be still

III. LAND

Under the Tremont fire light
with rugged Flintstone aliens
stun gunning for Barney
el diablo selling blarney
trying to get lit like the others
but he's a poor entrepreneur these days
getting gray and feeling in the way
like they feel to him

But before waxing grim
he orders another
Sam Adams draft
from the café owner
taking pleasure in the thought
that someone takes his orders
even if no one follows

I can't stop now
I'm on the verge of a major revelation
and I'm gonna share it
no matter whether you approve
as soon as I know what it is

Meanwhile we return
to the Flintstone aliens
wide eyed and warm on the rug
beneath the faux fireplace
affixed to the bar wall
while he awaits the inevitable
insatiable feet of poets
on his face and hands and
black abdomen that fades
into the textile background
making it appear as though

he is all eyes and gloved hands
and feet and green helmet

I can't stop now
I'm on the verge of a major revelation
but it is forty minutes after
the poetry reading was
set to begin and I'm out
of beer and still not in
and lit or not
my home soul
oar system
awaits

Art Achoke

I feel I need
to write more
but sometimes
I feel I talk too
much and the people
who listen already know
or misunderstand
and the people who don't
don't care anyway
and sometimes it's easier
to find and consume
busier work
and choke

Unwhet Dream

Covered with smashed
wild eyed pilgrims
masses of incomprehension

Yes just wants to get
out of their way

Soul percent of the city
under forced labor
fractured with unknowing

Brown cobweb languages
the only witnesses

Numb and Numbered
—*after* The Number 23

I see sequences of numbers in everything
Though nothing adds up
I see letters and code
What's been gained
What's owed
But what I thought I knew I knew
Makes as much sense to me now as
Two plus
Two equals
Five or
Six or
Six six six

An unseemly summation of my forty-odd years of
Cruel and/or kind
Clue blind
Calculations

An accurate accounting
Eludes me
Go figure

Number sequences in everything
Letters and code
What's been gained
What's owed
All adds up to any number you like
Or dislike
Multiplies and divides exponentially
Counting
Down
Days
To
A beastly human end

Ultimately six six six
And everything else
Adds up
To nothing

And nothing adds up

To infinity

Low Kay Shun
—after April Wine

If you see Kay
tell her I love her
miss her
wish she were on the menu.

If you see Kay
tell her I'm sorry
she's not allowed in this venue.

Not sure why
doesn't make much sense
might have something to do with religion
or the government.

Her friends Whore and War are welcome anytime
but if you see Kay
tell her no way!
She can't come.

Most everyone else
can come 'til they're dumb.

A few other folks are welcome as long as
they wear the acceptable contextual clothes.

Dick Van Dyke
can come as often as he likes
but buy him
own him
call him *my* Dick
and he's not welcome.

Billowy pussy willows
can blossom and blow as they wish

but own one
mention that "*My* pussy will O..."
you'll soon discover
that fair or bare or not
in this place
you're *puss*ona non grata.

My Ps and Qs and I
are free to come and go
and lie as often as we will.

But if you see Kay
tell her the powers that be
have had their fill of her
and swill like her
is barred from the menu
in this venue
by the men who'd rather
go home and sin
—*ew*—
while warning a word like you
to not intrude on their poetry
their peach
pity free
dumb of speech
in this low Kay shun.

Disciples

Clarence looked a little
like a rabbi
and taught us
to play truth
or dare and we
had no doubt
he knew best
how to do it
since he had
a beard and his
own apartment
and we were
just twelve.

Ahem (A Hymn)

Stand up, stand up for Jesus
while his father knees us in the nuts
plugs us in our butts
aims to please us or displease us
as the case may be
by leading us into paths
of unrighteousness
for his name's sake
never giving us a break
teaching us to take
more than we live
die more than we give.

It's the same stale story:
we distribute his excrement
in this world gone grim
and attribute the government
of this shit can to him.

To God be the gory
grating things he hath done.

The Beater of the Absurd

Aunt Onan
Art toe
Food fetish
Hart rose too ho
Training weal
Sealing fancy
Spin sigh cull
Jack bean imp pull
Uncle

Mark This

Doesn't matter if you laminate me
punch a hole in the end of me
create a neck on me
you can tie a pretty rope around

I don't care if you stick me
in Shakespeare
in Salinger or Dr. Seuss
leave me in some tedious tome
you intend to finish at some point
but never do
or pick your teeth with me
drop me thoughtlessly on the floor
for your puppy to chew

I'm the son
and heir
of tall trees who
though often abused and misused
have gladly given their hearts and bark
for the sake of warm homes and art

I'm much more
than a bookmark

Clothes 'n' Time

I sit in JC Penney waiting
for Merry to emerge
from the fitting room
me in a black pleather chair
arm rest torn
hole filled with
cottony stuffing soaked
with black magic
marker and a hope
I won't notice

She emerges with clothes
that would have been
two sizes too big last month
probably won't fit next month
and cost too much today

We finish
buy nothing after all
and I imagine myself
an afterthought
like the chair
she throws them in
or back on the rack
with the rest
of the clothes
hung up
dangling unowned
no longer subject
to wear and tear

Statuesque

Shiva dances before me
without moving
in a ring of flame
with no burning

On the shelf below him
clock hands bend
toward a cemented keyhole
one sixteen forever

Hand clock twist

Hour second merge

The illusion
grows hard
collects dust
as day dances on
in a ring of flame
still forever
by turns
cold
turgid
hopeful

Pa Tricked

—after "Lamb to the Slaughter" by Roald Dahl

You chopped a hunk
of bone and nougat from
the back of my head
and it fell face down
on your kitchen linoleum
looking like nothing
more than a hair glob
with a blood halo

I heard your snickers
from the other room
as the police gobbled
up your guilt with wool
over their eyes

When the shank in
their bellies is turned
to shit and long
forgotten
I'll imagine
you still
nuts about
me lamb
chop

Angler

You pretended
to befriend me
on Facebook
but you never
showed me
your real
face and you
said you were
a line pro
but you
would not share

Your real
work with me
was salty wet
crashing then
fishy

I wanted you
to keep
spinning out

You wanted
me too

Wave
goodbye

Unreel

Oct. Dawn

You looked far
too warm to have
a cold tonight

And when you
coughed during
my second poem

I craved your
phlegm all over
my body of work

Makes Her Mark

It took a while
for my knee to
attract yours
but when it did
the whole room
seemed to cream
and pulsate
turn reprobate
stiffen in well
lubricated laughter
raw and rhapsodic
as we bohemians
felt the downy heat
of our bourbon
Queen

Training Camp

My head hurts like a tear
in the fabric of my brain
like a locomotive hit it
at 80 miles per hour
like it's been
waterboarded by
the C.I.A. in an
undisclosed location
and it's all my fault

See I ate a hole
in my own heart
with half a dozen
mason jars of Green
Flash and it all
bled together

Again and again I lie
or dance on the rails
unattractive
waiting
for a cut in
half a chance
with my community
chest yearning
to be smashed
by enough Night Train
or be torn wide
with the untrained scythe
of my presumed immortality

Put me on my back
immobilize me
cover my face with a shroud
and pour another round

Pullet

Brian Eno's *Oblique Strategies*
are a deck of cards.

You pull one at random
when you want to be unstuck.

The one I pulled tonight
says "Use Filters."

So I took another taste
of my martini.

Unfinished

Here's the poem
I could not write.
Here's the night
I could not sleep.
Here too's the night
you could not keep faith.
Here's the wraith
jealousy taunting me.
Here's the wanting
I cannot fulfill.
Here's the hill
I cannot climb.
Here's the time
I mime my heart and flail.
Here's the failure
I've become.
Here's the numb
anger.
Here's the danger.
Here's the manger
where Jesus lies
a baby again.
Here's the sin
he will not grow
old again to die for.
Here's the why for
an eye for an eyesore
and a whore for more.
Here's the chore
I've become.
Here's the sum
of my unquiet
desperation.
Here's my need
for infinitely recurring validation.

Here's my long drawn out dissipation.
Here's my scattershot elation
smashed to feathers like a bird
on an Erie hotel window.
Here's the din roaring.
Here's the warring
I'm afraid to win
or engage in.
Here again
I simply could
not say no
except to what
I love most.
Here I'm toast
and the poem I could not
write is finished.
We are not.

A Cross Tic

Willing to
Inch its way
Loosely through
Ladles of
Inconspicuous
Alley trails,
Meters run out as
Suburbia worries,
Believing the
Universe can
Reach an end while
Revolving like doors
Over out and
Under in until
Glory comes
Holed up in bare
Sallow soupy flesh.

De-Carton
—for j/j

hastain
out rings
what would
box xyr in

to miss pique
say has stain
or limit by
pronoun
might reveal
a vision gap
or dirty need
to punch holes
without consent

think about it

let beauty be
indelible

love being
stop boxing

LadySings

Through blue headache
my words come hard
Colt 45 to my lips
I pull its trigger
feel the spill
down my throat.

Her words and hers
come easier
taste better
give greater relief
inspire envy in
Billy Dee Williams.

Suite Melissa

In my city of lost places
Melissa is on the ventilator
a year to the day after
Geri was removed
and I will not know
for two more days

It was just two
weeks ago she declined
to attend my Sandusky reading
because she had pneumonia
when she did not
know it was really stage four
lung cancer

In my city of lost places
they are now removing her
breathing tube and I have not
seen Melissa since 2004
at a corner store on Prospect
in Elyria and we have not
comingled since
more than ten years
before that

It was just too
difficult with one of us
in prison then both of us
married to admit ourselves
emotionally conjoined since
she had been my first
turn on to poetry
King Crimson and LSD

In my city of lost places
I remember her
telling me about her
dead twin Vanessa
who she claimed to be
while pretending
Melissa was the one
who had died in infancy

It was just two
sides of one woman though
like the one who made her children
stay in their room so I could
put her ankles next to her ears
several years after the one
who had bloodied my back
in childless ecstasy

In my city of lost places
I want to go see her
before she is no more
but for the past year
after she sent an out
of nowhere card
to Geri's funeral
she's been afraid for me
to see her in person
instead merely mailing me
a twelve year old photo
to scan and return
and anyway I don't want to
make anything more difficult

In my city of lost places
a poem that will do Melissa
justice eludes me
so alone I play my favorite
Allman Brothers song on repeat
remember the advent of my poetry
and mourn the imminent over
and over

Mastering Ascension

It's easy
for a man
to believe
in ascension
when he's erect.

It's hard
when he's not.

Mr. Testosterone

A sunny vegetarian
wowed the Missouri
audience with her
poem about taxidermy

while he kept
thinking about eating
and mounting her.

My Me Mine

I'm going inside
hoping to be a lantern
not a canary.

Booking

I want to follow
my obsessions

literarily at least
as Christian Bök

recommends
but I feel crazy

taking advice
from a Christian.

Half Write

T.S. Eliot
said poetry
is not
a career.

He was only
half right.

It is not
a car
but it is
an ear.

Careering

The guy in the Scion
in front of me has a
license plate that reads
CABBAGE.

He should've been
a taxi driver.

Birther

If life begins
at conception
we celebrate
Christmas
nine months late.

Sibyl

—after *Portrait of an Astrologer in a White Dress* by Herbert Ascherman, Jr.

Aries is my brother
building an illegal bonfire
in his suburban back yard.

Taurus is my mother,
the origin of my poesy,
bequeathing me her
incongruous bull horns.

Gemini is a roller coaster,
mirror hook and grommet,
full soar and plummet.

Cancer nips at my back.

Leo is a manely masseuse
loosing regal courage
where and when I least expect.

Virgo is an exacting secret.

Libra scales a mountain of excrement,
finding balance at its summit.

Scorpio is my adoptive father
stinging the air,
my bottom now
out of reach.

Sagittarius prances deftly
over my head, a thought balloon
keeping would-be backstabbers at bay.

Capricorn philosophizes disaster away.

Aquarius yearns to be a fortunate oasis.

Pisces fishes
for homeostasis.

And they all revolve
around me, the astrologer,
brilliant in my white dress,
gleaning relationship
and illumination
from the universal night.

From Genesis to Exodus
—after Prince Rogers Nelson*

In the beginning
there was God
and God was much more
than a B-side
to Purple Rain
the single before
I Would Die 4 U

God was the one I called
faggot in high school
several years before
I knew better
and became a true believer
and knew I was pansexual

God was ubiquitous on MTV
the summer I entered
the Marine Corps at 17
and exited the Marine Corps
still 17
dazed
U're gonna have to fight
Ur own damn war

God was there
purple on screen
during my first blow job
at Tower Drive-In
and he was always

there on my clock radio
in Wilkes Villa
seen and known
on scene and unknowable
in my homeless backpack
in Cascade Park
plugged into
the table cassette player
at the LCCC library
and in the background
as I went down for the first time
on Cassie's *raspberry* hooray

God was still there
a prince of a man
as I made it through college
cut off my wannabe Jheri curl
took a job at the gay bar
lost and found my identi-tease
again and again and even when
through enforced sobriety
and concrete cell walls
I watched 1999 come and go
and raved *un2 the joy*
monastic

Joan Osborne asked *what if*
God was one of us?
and he was
and he walked among us
and often we knew him not
especially when he became Jehovah's witness
and exorcised his songs from You Tube
and bought into chemtrail conspiracy theories

Percocet pantomimes and a Fentanyl flatline
because living can be painful
even when you're God
especially when you're God

And in the 21st century God was still
here with us
even as TMZ declared him dead
and though I live
on Alphabet Street
no psalm of mine
can capture his new power
glory

I love U more than I did
when U were mine

[*The italicized phrases in this poem, even that by
Joan Osborne, come from songs Prince recorded.]

Unfounded

In this city of lost places
my fifteen-year-old granddaughter
is no longer hiding
all the places she cuts
herself to hide
all the places
she hurts.

I imagine it's because she does not
want to die
and the cutting makes her
feel alive
or because she feels
dead inside
or like—hell
I can only speculate why
because she cannot
tell.

In my city of lost places
there are six urns—
two wooden boxes
a metal canister
and three fancier ones
from the funeral home—
full of ashes and bone bits
our dogs Lucky and Lady
her eighteen-year-old cat Cricket
my mother-in-law
sister-in-law Sheree
and wife Geri Lynne
because I cannot bear
to bury them.

In my city of lost places

there is a light that never goes out
and there is an out that never gets lit
and there is a fit that never gets fought
and there is an it that never gets
sought or wrought

In my city of lost places
the oyster is my world
until it is not anymore
and still sometimes is and there is
a this that cannot be that
and there is an at
that cannot be bliss
and it seems all things
are hurting and healing
and feeling like cutting themselves.

In my city of lost places
a seamstress has come undone
a teacher has failed to master the lesson
and a doctor has caught his death.

I imagine it's because she does not
want to live
and the cutting makes her
feel dead
or loved inside
or like—hell
I can only speculate
and expectorate why
when I do
not know.

In my city of lost places
it's the first anniversary
of my wife's death
her clothing is still in our dresser
and hanging in my closet
and the black framed family

photo collage from her
hospital room still
sits in my living room
on her former make-up table
and her make-up is still
in my bathroom with her tweezers
and scissors and razor
and whatever has not yet been cut
is torn apart
and I feel her
with me and not
and realize sometimes it's easier
to love your mate unconditionally
when she no longer expects
anything of you.

Twilight
—*after Diego Rivera's* Evening Twilight at Acapulco

Distance howls, doglike,
on a darkening ocean
as my bark founders.

Immersion

A river runs through Lorain
on the day of grandson Marcus' birthday,
the day before Dad's wedding anniversary,
the day after niece Maddy's death anniversary,
a day or two after Yule,
a week or three after Hanukkah
and two days before Christmas.
Reliably brown and stodgy, older
than all those so-called holidays,
the river is always moving, evolving,
devolving on its way to Lake
Erie from the heart of Ohio.
It is never the same stream though
my eyes would not know it
without me throwing a pebble in
and watching the Black River
splash while I feel a shiver wash over
me and contemplate drowning.

Judge Marks

In the name of your Bible
expecting America
to buy your bull.

In the name of Jesus
confirming a devil
to the Supreme Court.

In the name of the Father
distressing women since
at least high school.

In the name of the Holy Spirit
drinking unholy Bro-weiser
leaving indelible bruises.

No Other

—*after* Far Enemy *by Tony Ingrisano*

A wide web of geometry and pixelation
looms over my brick suburban bungalow.

The colors warm and entice me
with creeping florescent sophistication.

I feel them drawing me up and in
while equally I am drawing them inside.

It's a network of jasmine attraction
bringing untoward craving and resentment,

hate and cruelty from America the beautiful,
Russian bots, unacknowledged racists,

television networks, Amazon.com, nihilism
proponents, penile enhancement specialists,

trolls, moles, sexist pols and ad-mongers,
while the colors of it all bleed into pools

of need and reaction, stupefaction,
failure to listen disguised as debate,

hasty action, dystopian dissatisfaction,
snark disguised as lark, and warring factions.

This poem began as an expression of appreciation
for a wide web of precious colors and pixelation

before I met the so-called far enemies
in my bathroom mirror and hardly

recognized them as something other
than other.

Lens

[Cues in brackets not meant to be read aloud]

Chorus:

VIOLENCE   silence

violence   SILENCE

A. Verse:

Less is more and more is less and silence
is most golden to the rich and oppressive
and would be impressive if not for the give
gone missing from nature's desired balance

Give and take and
give and take and
give and
    take and
    take and
    take and
    take *[make a scratching sound
as though roughly removing the needle]*

The record keeps skipping
time to pull out the needle

Chorus:

VIOLENCE   silence

violence   SILENCE

Stuck in the same groove

B. Verse:

Sometimes I feel like an acquisition
infected by a controlbot
running as my masters intend
whenever anyone sticks coins into my slot
like I'm programmed
to consume and consume
subsume
take a nap
and resume
consume subsume

Size matters
bigger is better
stronger faster
forget impending disaster
I want to be the sixty million dollar man
when I grow down

Can't wake up
need to drink more coffee

Can't go to sleep
need to drink more wine

Always hungry
need more mine
all the time in between

Never satisfied
I dine and dine
on more and more swine

prove the proverb true

I am what I eat
maybe you are too

Chorus:

VIOLENCE   silence

violence   SILENCE

Distinction blurs

C. Verse:

Kill 'em all and let God sort 'em out

We human would-be gods
can't wait to start sorting
the money and land and command
the dead leave behind
but first we need your ass *[cough]* assistance

Be all that you can be
join
consume
follow
consume
collect
consume
kill
consume
die
consumed

Submission accomplished

Chorus:

VIOLENCE   silence

violence   SILENCE

D. Coda:

Contract the compound
distill its essence
sigh, violence
vie, silence
contract it further
vi... 'ce
vi...'se

You can spell it either way
with an S or a C
violence silence
vi... 'ce
vi...'se
vice vise baby
the record keeps skipping
the handle keeps turning

The head I've been helping
to squeeze is my own
and my children's

Time to pull out the needle
stop churning the handle
look in a mirror
for a moment
put my vy-
ing and my sigh-
ing aside
and focus
my lens.

Judas Priest

My name is not Frankie Lee
and Dylan never sang about me.

I'm locked, loaded and strapped
though my only weapon is my voice.

I'm no longer hell bent for leather
or screaming for vengeance

though my jacket might look the part.
It is made of polyester fibers and heart.

And though I often wear motorcycle boots
I've long outgrown two-wheeled passions

and I no longer call myself a victim of changes
since I learned to embrace their inevitability.

I'm a bi polar rocka rolla turbo
painkiller with stained class.

But if you think my sad wings
of destiny make me a killing machine

you've got another thing coming.

Ataraxis

—after Equanimity *by Dana Oldfather*

incline into
equanimity
earth blood
green mud
recline into
infinity
be bud
be home
be om
namo bhagavate vasudevaya
insh'allah wah
there is no
there is know sew
be bloom
be lilt
be boom
be wilt
heal merry
full of grays
judge nothing
black or white
more or less
all calm
nam myoho renge kyo
hello good why
sway marigold
do chai tea
sip t'ai chi
I knead know
need no dough
no mantra

am not I
we are eye
are know
need no labels
seek not
need not find
untangle ataraxis
un-angle collapse
not without feeling
flowing into serenity
simple complexity
complex simplicity
simply see
and be
equanimity

Kruhaus: A Quarterly Gathering

Tonight in the Den of Verity
at Hooked on Colfax
poets will fire introspections
burn misconceptions and
foment resurrections.

Stay tuned
for flaming postcards
from the conflagration.

Leda off Leash at Creekside Cottage in Athens, Ohio

Freedom's just
another word
for natural
boundaries on
three sides
and a cedar
fence on the
fourth to keep her
from running
into the road.

Rough Cure

The woman with medicine in her voice
placed her head in my lap like a cat.

I heard her purr over that of my supercharged engine
as my foot pushed the accelerator deeper.

I wanted her to unbuckle my inhibitions
but she had higher ambitions.

She wanted to heal me. However,
I am a dog not easily brought to heel.

Like July

Once in a violet heart moon
a woman appears—in cold March—
reading poems that I call beautiful—
a trite word I use by default because
her presence is more poetic than
the most flowery words I can muster.

Once in a post-valentine dream
a woman appears who makes the whole room
each fragment of my shattered heart
—I want to say the world entire—
less painful and much warmer.

Luster

I am starstruck
by an apparition
wearing mostly black,
a compelling blend of light
and shadow, inspiring
dream schemes beyond
the realm of routine,
starstruck by another chance
or a fantasy that one can dance
whole out of overcast April
while Spring continues to unveil
her splendor,
starstruck by once faraway
rays that wake the day and
animate my clay star stuff,
making this long darkened
everything begin again
to glow.

Alack
—*after Issa*

In lieu of my usual evening
at home *BoJack Horseman* binge
I sit on my sofa and pine for a woman
who would probably be best off not
to pine back. And yet....

And yet....

Hampuy ("Come")
—*after Catherine Joslyn's* Luminous Threads *exhibition**

the Woman of Blessing flies by
and lizard Eye calls her Goddess
as my shadow self nips at my right
rear foot and though I am
skeptical of anything called
supernatural She assures me
magic is afoot
in the wind

as far as the venom goes
those that follow will be
reinvented with glowing
frog hearts purple heart beats
brown eyes with purple pupils
raining glitter down

come back to the place
where You've always belonged

the Woman of Blessing is undressing
myth and history sharing *Her*story
speaking to me in Quechua
and sometimes in Spanish
and remains near even when
She appears to vanish

She could be Hungarian
Italian, African, Arabic
Hebrew, *She*brew too
as She transcends limitation
like You
and even You
if only You knew

borders are for colonists
ingrates and inmates
hates
not Blessings

from the Incan *wakatay*
to Your tastebuds
to the Lakota's *Wakan Tanka*
to Your best buds
to Frank Zappa's *Waka/Jawaka*
and Bing's "Mississippi Mud"
the Great Spirit takes many forms
transcends definition
and blood

Jamie sees "I Last" in her shower-
steamed bathroom mirror and
attributes it to her mother my wife
while Paul Manafort enters a plea
deal to cooperate in Russiagate
and Dave sends me a book signed
by longtime hero Allen Ginsberg
and Shelley turns RJ's million tomatoes
into sauce and salsa before they rot
and Dianne has already produced a poem
as good as or better than mine
in a fraction of the time
and Leda my dog is happy just to leave
our house and accompany me to
the Tradesman Tavern in Parma
where I drink Great Lakes and
continue to contemplate
Cathie Joslyn's art
and Andean-inspired textiles
Shamans and lizards
and She and all They
and often You too
are or can be
the Woman of Blessing

whatever Your gender

come back to the place
where You've always belonged

lizard Eye sees only "i as"
In the mirror while the Woman
of Blessing keeps flying by
next in the form of Rita Dove
her *Grace Notes* and more nestled
on my attic shelves between Dougherty's
The Second O of Sorrow and
Doyle's Sherlock Holmes mysteries
I pull out Rita's *Collected Poems*
read her inscription written two
years ago today on my not-yet-late wife's
60th birthday offering me "every good
wish on your 50th" which would be
three days later

somehow it all continues
to come together even
when I feel pain
and there's no
Easter resurrection
still life and energy
remain like magic
afoot in the air

the dance moves of another
planet are waiting for Your hair
to wrap itself around sparkly
tendrils with luminous entanglement
and then dive into the gurgling
above ground water join
forces with friendly amphibians

as far as the venom goes

those who follow will be
reimagined as lightbearers
with glowing frog entrails
in which glorious potentialities
might be seen

come back to the place
where You've always belonged

from the Incan *wakatay*
to Your taste buds
from the Lakota's *Wakan Tanka*
to Your best buds
to Frank Zappa's *Waka/Jawaka*
and Bing's "Mississippi Mud"
earth/time Mother
Incan *Pachamama*
the Great Spirit
takes many forms
transcends definition
and blood
and is not
necessarily supernatural
though She appears to be

She is earth and wind
and You and every Woman
of Blessing You meet and Matter
and Everything that matters
can never be destroyed or created
no matter the venom or storm
but merely take on different forms
or appearances of form
even when formless
borderless because borders
are for colonists
ingrates and inmates
hates and reprobates

unlike We who strive instead
to be Great Spirits blessing
Each Other and Our world
a Happy Flying Woman
ever present *Pachamama*
wind Shaman planet Goddess
praying down good will
upon Our shadow selves
scurrying as lizards across
scorched earth thirsting
for a Blessing We cannot
see or seize though it is
already Ours
each Breath
We take
and give
each moment
We live

come back to the place
where You've always belonged

[*This poem incorporates a dozen or so lines by Juliet Cook]

Odd Missive

Dear whomever it may concern
I have always felt upside down
and downside up
like an hourglass
or a cup tumbling
down a mountain of valleys
like an alley full of endless avenues
and dead-end streets
like a meet-up nobody comes to
or a voice recorder in a landfill
I have always felt
like a number one Diana Ross
song on my fourteenth birthday
Upside Down
but also sometimes
her subsequent single
I'm Coming Out
I have always felt outside in
and insight out
but never insight in
unless I'm mistaken
or outside out
unless my heart was breaking
and I could no longer bear the indoors.
I have always felt
like a rooftop floor
or a basement ceiling
like a numb feeling
or the unreeling business
of a word-proof letter
like an un-gotten go getter
a colander filled with holy water
like an arid pants wetter
a desert detour
an albino Moor

the kind of hello
who is talking to himself again
to whomever it may concern
even when
it concerns only him
or not even.

How odd.

Sincerely,
Miss Sieve

John Burroughs

About the author

John Burroughs of Cleveland (Ohio) is the **2019-2021 Ohio Beat Poet Laureate**. Playwright, musician, editor, and the author of a dozen previous poetry collections, John is a dynamic performer who has wowed audiences from Oakland to New York City and myriad points in between.

He hosts the monthly **Poetry+** reading series at **Art on Madison** in Lakewood, Ohio, and has served since 2008 as the founding editor for **Crisis Chronicles Press**, publishing over one hundred books by esteemed writers from around the world.

Find him on Facebook, Twitter (@jesuscrisis) or at www.crisischronicles.com.

He is also a founding member of the Rolling Stock troupe of poets.

Acknowledgments

The author is grateful and in many cases deeply indebted to the following, in which some of these poems, often in earlier versions, first appeared:

Bloggerel (2008, Crisis Chronicles Press)
6/9: Improvisations in Dependence (2009, Crisis Chronicles Press)
Identity Crises (2009, Green Panda Press)
Electric Company (2011, Writing Knights Press)
Water Works (2012, recycled karma press)
Lens (2012, Crisis Chronicles Press)
The Eater of the Absurd (2012, NightBallet Press)
Barry Merry Baloney (2012, Spare Change Press)
It Takes More than Chance to Make Change (2013, Poet's Haven)
Oct Tongue – 1 (2014, Crisis Chronicles Press)
Beat Attitude (2015, NightBallet Press)
A Case for Ascension (2015, Asinimali Press)
Water Works (2017, Poet's Haven)
Loss and Foundering (2018, NightBallet Press)

48th Street Press broadside series, *The Artistic Muses*, *BEAT-itude: National Beat Poetry Festival 10 Year Anthology*, *Big Hammer*, *blackdahlia*, *Buzzkill: Apocalypse* [NightBallet], *Cartier Street Review*, *The City Poetry*, *Common Threads*, *Crisis Chronicles Cyber Litmag*, *Delirious: A Poetic Celebration of Prince* [NightBallet], *Erbacce*, *Eviscerator Heaven*, *Force Fed*, *Gasconade Review*, Green Panda Press monthly digest, *Guerilla Pamphlets*, *Heights Observer*, several volumes of the annual *Hessler Street Fair Poetry Anthology*, *Hip Poetry*, *Lake Effect Poetry 2014 & 2015 Team Anthology*, Le Pink-Elephant Press bookmark series, *Lief Magazine*, *Lipsmack: A Sampler Platter of Poets from NightBallet Press*, *The Long Islander*, *Mnemosyne*, *The Nexxuss*, *NEO Poets Field Guide*, NightBallet Press broadside series, *The Passion in Pink*, *Pine Mountain Sand & Gravel*, *The*

Poetry of S.O.U.L., *Poet's Haven* podcast, *Poets to Come, Polarity, Pudding Magazine, Rosebud, Rounding of the Stone, Rubicon: Words & Art Inspired by Oscar Wilde's De Profundis, Rusty Truck, SDA Art Tract #1, Shake the Tree Anthology – Volume 2* [Brightly Press], *Ship of Fools, South Florida Poetry Journal, The Squire, Troubadour 21, Vending Machine: Poetry for Change, Water Me Well* anthology, *We Are Beat: National Beat Poetry Foundation Anthology, What I Knew Before I Knew: Poems from the Pudding House Salon-Cleveland, While You Were Sleeping I Dreamt a Poem: Cleveland Salon 2013 Anthology, Winedrunk Sidewalk, Red Heart:Black Heart* [Writer's Digest], *Writers Reading* podcast, *Writing Knights Press 2011 Anthology* and assorted exhibitions at Art on Madison and Heights Arts in Greater Cleveland.

CPSIA information can be obtained
at www.ICGtesting.com
Printed in the USA
LVHW092324190819
628258LV00001B/13/P